# THE PASSION TRANSLATION

## THE PASSIONATE LIFE BIBLE STUDY SERIES

12-LESSON STUDY GUIDE

THE BOOK OF

# PSALMS

### PART ONE
The Psalms of Joy

*poetry on fire*

**BroadStreet**
PUBLISHING

BroadStreet Publishing® Group, LLC
Savage, Minnesota, USA
BroadStreetPublishing.com

TPT The Book of Psalms – Part 1: 12-Lesson Study Guide
Copyright © 2023 BroadStreet Publishing Group

9781424564415 (softcover)
9781424564422 (ebook)

Stock or custom editions of BroadStreet Publishing titles may be purchased in bulk for educational, business, ministry, fundraising, or sales promotional use. For information, please email orders@broadstreetpublishing.com.

General editor: Brian Simmons
Managing editor: William D. Watkins
Writer: Christy Phillippe

Design and Typesetting by Garborg Design Works | garborgdesign.com

Printed in China

23 24 25 26 27 5 4 3 2 1

# Contents

# From God's Heart to Yours

"God is love," says the apostle John, and "Everyone who loves is fathered by God and experiences an intimate knowledge of him" (1 John 4:7). The life of a Christ-follower is, at its core, a life of love—God's love of us, our love of him, and our love of others and ourselves because of God's love for us.

And this divine love is reliable, trustworthy, unconditional, other-centered, majestic, forgiving, redemptive, patient, kind, and more precious than anything else we can ever receive or give. It characterizes each person of the Trinity—Father, Son, and Holy Spirit—and so is as limitless as they are. They love one another with this eternal love, and they reach beyond themselves to us, created in their image with this love.

How do we know such incredible truths? Through the primary source of all else we know about the one God—his Word, the Bible. Of course, God reveals who he is through other sources as well, such as the natural world, miracles, our inner life, our relationships (especially with him), those who minister on his behalf, and those who proclaim him to us and others. But the fullest and most comprehensive revelation we have of God and from him is what he has given us in the thirty-nine books of the Hebrew Scriptures (the Old Testament) and the twenty-seven books of the Christian Scriptures (the New Testament). Together, these sixty-six books present a compelling and telling portrait of God and his dealings with us.

It is these Scriptures that *The Passionate Life Bible Study Series* is all about. Through these study guides, we—the editors and writers of this series—seek to provide you with a unique and welcoming opportunity to delve more deeply into God's precious Word, encountering there his loving heart for you and all the others he loves. God wants you to know him more deeply, to love him more devoutly, and to share his heart with others more frequently and freely. To accomplish this, we have based this study guide series on The Passion Translation of the Bible, which strives to "reintroduce the passion and fire of the Bible to the English reader. It doesn't merely convey the literal meaning of words. It expresses God's passion for people and his world by translating the original, life-changing message of God's Word for modern readers." It has been created to "kindle in you a burning desire to know the heart of God, while impacting the church for years to come."[1]

In each study guide, you will find an introduction to the Bible book it covers. There you will gain information about that Bible book's authorship, date of composition, first recipients, setting, purpose, central message, and key themes. Each lesson following the introduction will take a portion of that Bible book and walk you through it so you will learn its content better while experiencing and applying God's heart for your own life and encountering ways you can share his heart with others. Along the way, you will come across a number of features we have created that provide opportunities for more life application and growth in biblical understanding.

 ## Experience God's Heart

This feature focuses questions on personal application. It will help you live out God's Word and to bring the Bible into your world in fresh, exciting, and relevant ways.

 ## Share God's Heart

This feature will help you grow in your ability to share with other people what you learn and apply in a given lesson. It provides guidance on using the lesson to grow closer to others and to enrich your fellowship with others. It also points the way to enabling you to better listen to the stories of others so you can bridge the biblical story with their stories.

**The Backstory**

This feature provides ancient historical and cultural background that illuminates Bible passages and teachings. It deals with then-pertinent religious groups, communities, leaders, disputes, business trades, travel routes, customs, nations, political factions, ancient measurements and currency...in short, anything historical or cultural that will help you better understand what Scripture says and means.

 **Word Wealth**

This feature provides definitions for and other illuminating information about key terms, names, and concepts, and how different ancient languages have influenced the biblical text. It also provides insight into the different literary forms in the Bible, such as prophecy, poetry, narrative history, parables, and letters, and how knowing the form of a text can help you better interpret and apply it. Finally, this feature highlights the most significant passages in a Bible book. You may be encouraged to memorize these verses or keep them before you in some way so you can actively hide God's Word in your heart.

 **Digging Deeper**

This feature explains the theological significance of a text or the controversial issues that arise and mentions resources you can use to help you arrive at your own conclusions. Another way to dig deeper into the Word is by looking into the life of a biblical character or another person from church history, showing how that man or woman incarnated a biblical truth or passage. For instance, Jonathan Edwards was well known for his missions work among native American Indians and for his intellectual prowess in articulating the Christian faith, Florence Nightingale for the reforms she brought about in healthcare, Irenaeus for his fight against heresy, Billy Graham for his work in evangelism, Moses for the strength God gave him to lead the Hebrews and receive and communicate the law, and Deborah for her work as a judge in Israel. This feature introduces to you figures from the past who model what it looks like to experience God's heart and share his heart with others.

##  The Extra Mile

While The Passion Translation's notes are extensive, sometimes students of Scripture like to explore more on their own. In this feature, we provide you with opportunities to glean more information from a Bible dictionary, a Bible encyclopedia, a reliable Bible online tool, another ancient text, and the like. Here you will learn how you can go the extra mile on a Bible lesson. And not just in study either. Reflection, prayer, discussion, and applying a passage in new ways provide even more opportunities to go the extra mile. Here you will find questions to answer and applications to make that will require more time and energy from you—if and when you have them to give.

As you can see above, each of these features has a corresponding icon so you can quickly and easily identify them.

You will find other helps and guidance through the lessons of these study guides, including thoughtful questions, application suggestions, and spaces for you to record your own reflections, answers, and action steps. Of course, you can also write in your own journal, notebook, computer document, or other resource, but we have provided you with space for your convenience.

Also, each lesson will direct you toward the introductory material and numerous notes provided in The Passion Translation. There each Bible book contains a number of aids supplied to help you better grasp God's words and his incredible love, power, knowledge, plans, and so much more. We want you to get the most out of your Bible study, especially using it to draw you closer to the One who loves you most.

Finally, at the end of each lesson you'll find a section called "Talking It Out." This contains questions and exercises for application that you can share, answer, and apply with your spouse, a friend, a coworker, a Bible study group, or any other individuals or groups who would like to walk with you through this material. As Christians, we gather together to serve, study, worship, sing, evangelize, and a host of other activities. We grow together, not just on our own. This section will give you ample opportunities to engage others with some of the content of each lesson so you can work it out in community.

We offer all of this to support you in becoming an even more faithful and loving disciple of Jesus Christ. A disciple in the ancient world was a student of her teacher, a follower of his master. Students study, and followers follow. Jesus' disciples are to sit at his feet and listen and learn and then do what he tells them and shows them to do. We have created *The Passionate Life Bible Study Series* to help you do what a disciple of Jesus is called to do.

So go.

Read God's words.

Hear what he has to say in them and through them.

Meditate on them.

Hide them in your heart.

Display their truths in your life.

Share their truths with others.

Let them ignite Jesus' passion and light in all you say and do.

Use them to help you fulfill what Jesus called his disciples to do: "Now wherever you go, make disciples of all nations, baptizing them in the name of the Father, the Son, and the Holy Spirit. And teach them to faithfully follow all that I have commanded you. And never forget that I am with you every day, even to the completion of this age" (Matthew 28:19–20).

And through all of this, let Jesus' love nourish your heart and allow that love to overflow into your relationships with others (John 15:9–13). For it was for love that Jesus came, served, died, rose from the dead, and ascended into heaven. This love he gives us. And this love he wants us to pass along to others.

# Why I Love Joy in the
# Book of Psalms

Songs of *joy* fill the Psalms and stir my soul! I love the book of Psalms because it brings me to the fountain of joy. Every time I read them, I feel like I'm having a divine encounter. David's melodies make me glad. Even when he was depressed, David (and all the authors of the Psalms) gave thanks to God. In a cave or in a castle, David learned to praise the Lord and walk in joy.

Here are some examples of joy in the Psalms:

> Because of you, I know the path of life,
> as I taste the fullness of joy in your presence.
> At your right side I experience divine pleasures
> forevermore!
> (16:11)

> But let them all be glad,
> those who turn aside to hide themselves in you.
> May they keep shouting for joy forever!
> Overshadow them in your presence as they sing
> and rejoice.
> Then every lover of your name will burst forth
> with endless joy.
> Lord, how wonderfully you bless the righteous.
> Your favor wraps around each one and covers
> them under your canopy of kindness and joy.
> (5:11–12)

> May your priests wear the robes of righteousness,
> and let all your godly lovers sing for joy!
> (132:9)

Yes, it's hard to sing if you don't have joy. But when the joy of the Lord fills your soul, songs of gladness will break forth. Even when life is difficult and the days seem long and lonely, there is a joy waiting for you in this book.

It's amazing how the Psalms speak to our lives today. Perhaps the central reason is that they are poems written in first person, that is, from the point of view of "I," "my," and "me." Because of this, whenever I open them again, I immediately find a human voice there, a voice that's crystal clear. The "I" is living a very rich life, full of physical, spiritual, and emotional extremes. And this "I" is strikingly honest, sharing life's ups and downs as well as personal feelings, thoughts, pleas, and praise. And no matter what comes out, these poems express a deep longing to be near God. This relationship with God has endless facets that move me because nothing is held back: frustration, struggle, joy, trust, praise. It's all there.

The Psalms echo the joy Jesus brings into our lives. I know you will find that glorious fountain of joy in these inspired lyrics. God's love, peace, and joy are waiting for you, so lift up your heart today and get ready to make a joyful noise!

Brian Simmons
General Editor

## LESSON 1

# Welcome to the Book of Psalms

Let everyone everywhere join in the crescendo
of ecstatic praise to Yahweh!
Hallelujah! Praise the Lord!

—PSALM 150:6

A passionate relationship with God is the heart-cry of every person, but many of us don't know how to express our praise, our prayers, our passion to God. When we face times of heartbreak, jubilation, confusion, loss, or thanksgiving, it may be difficult to find the words to share our thoughts and feelings with the Lord in prayer. The book of Psalms is a help and a comfort to all of us, for it allows us to pray and praise along with the writers as they express the deepest longings of their hearts and the most exuberant worship and thanks for God's amazing work in their lives.

The book of Psalms is a model of praise and prayer that we can follow. In fact, many believers have prayed through the Psalms, making the passages their own as they use them to speak to God and listen for his voice back to them. Psalms is a collection of different groups of prayers and songs used by the people of God for centuries, beginning in Old Testament times. The word "psalms" comes from the Greek word *psalmos*, translated from the Hebrew word *mizmor*, which means "songs" or "a poem set to notes."[2] In the centuries before Jesus was born, the psalms helped a largely illiterate population learn and remember God's Word by setting his words to music. They also played a critical role in the community as the people came together to worship God in the temple as well as in the many synagogues.

- *Have you ever had trouble finding the words to express your thoughts and feelings to God or difficulty putting language to your heart's deepest feelings and concerns? Describe a time or two that this occurred.*

- *Did you find a way to get past this time? What did you do and learn from it?*

# Authorship

The psalms were composed by a number of people who lived in Old Testament times: David wrote seventy-three of the psalms; his son, King Solomon, wrote two of them. Other authors include Asaph, the sons of Korah, Jeduthun, Heman, Etan, and Moses. They were collected over centuries, but most were written between the time of David's reign (ca. 1000 BC) and Ezra's ministry (ca. 450 BC).

The book of Psalms that we have in our Bibles today is a collection that is divided into five sub-collections, or books, which seem to relate to the Pentateuch—the first five books of the Hebrew Old Testament. The Pentateuch is a book of instruction for God's people, just as the book of Psalms is a kind of instruction manual on worshiping God and going to him with our joys and sorrows.

A popular phrase some years ago provoked thought about "What would Jesus do?"—enabling believers to consider different options when they faced confusion in life or had to make important decisions. As we read the book of Psalms, we could consider the question "How would David pray?" when we need help expressing our thoughts and feelings to the Lord.

- *Have you ever used one or more of the psalms in the Bible to express your feelings to God? If so, what was the result? If you have not, do you think this would help you as you engage with God in prayer? In what ways?*

# Key Themes

The book of Psalms is a book of poetry. It is often interpreted differently from other books in the Bible, such as a book of history (like Genesis or Judges) or a letter of Paul (like Romans or Titus). Poetry uses fluid language, including metaphors and poetic techniques that are not usually meant to be taken literally. The Psalms express deep emotion, and readers can utilize them in a devotional way. Still, different psalms had different uses for the original worshipers, and they have different uses for us today. Many psalms are hymns of praise, in which we join the writer in acknowledging the greatness and the majesty of our God. Some are psalms of lament, in which we express our sorrow for sin, a request for God to intervene in our life circumstances, a desire to see his enemies punished, or a plea to him for help. Other psalms include songs of thanksgiving, while wisdom psalms teach or instruct God's people. Many psalms were songs that God's community sang as they gathered for worship.

# 𝕹 WORD WEALTH

The Hebrew word *selah* is found throughout the book of Psalms. Many people believe that it indicates a place to stop and think about what has just been read or spoken aloud. The translator of The Passion Translation has used the phrase "pause in his presence" to indicate where this phrase is used in the Psalms. Here is what he says about the translation of this word:

> The Hebrew word *Selah* [is] a puzzling word to translate. Most scholars believe it is a musical term for pause or rest. It is used seventy-one times in the Psalms as an instruction to the music leader to pause and ponder in God's presence. An almost identical word, *Sela*, means

"a massive rock cliff." It is said that when *Selah* is spoken, the words are carved in stone in the throne room of the heavens.[3]

As you pause in God's presence throughout this study, consider how he also pauses to listen to you.

## A Mirror into Our Souls

The book of Psalms is a beautiful, eloquent collection of patterns for prayer. Essentially, in Psalms, prayer has been married to poetry, and it is here that we find expression for all the emotions of life. The church father Athanasius wrote this about the book of Psalms: "The psalms seem to me to be like a mirror, in which one can see himself and the stirrings of his own heart; he can recite them against the background of his own emotions."[4] And John Calvin wrote this about Psalms, calling it "an anatomy of parts of the soul":

> There is not an emotion of which anyone can be conscious that is not here represented as in a mirror. Or rather, the Holy Spirit has here drawn to the life all the griefs, sorrows, fears, doubts, hopes, cares, perplexities, in short, all the distracting emotions with which the minds of men are wont to be agitated.[5]

• *What is your favorite psalm? Why?*

# EXPERIENCE GOD'S HEART

Any good relationship requires a give-and-take in communication. One person talks, and another person listens and responds. The entire Bible is made up of God's Word to us. We listen to his words, learn from his teaching, and consider the lives of God's people who have gone before us. Now, the book of Psalms adds a dimension to this that the other books of Scripture do not. In Psalms, we hear God's people using words to reach out to the Lord. Other books contain divine encounters and some occasional prayers, but no other book of the Bible solely comprises prayers and praises to God as Psalms does. Consequently, through this book we can learn how to respond to God and answer his words to us. His Word is not meant for us to simply read and then set aside; we are to answer him in prayer and in actions as we pursue a personal relationship with him that fulfills the deepest longings of our heart.

- *What deep emotions have you struggled to express to God in the past?*

- *How do you anticipate the book of Psalms helping you with your prayer life and your worship of the Lord?*

## ❤ SHARE GOD'S HEART

Praise and worship to God are meant not only to be individual efforts but also to be a community undertaking. The same is true of prayer. It surely is important to cultivate your own times of prayer and worship with the Lord, but we must also not neglect gathering together for times of prayer, praise, worship, and collective petitioning for the needs of one another and those still outside of Christ.

- *How does your experience of prayer and worship differ when you are alone and when you are gathered together with other believers?*

- *Is there someone in your life who is struggling with his or her relationship with God? How might the book of Psalms be a comfort to that person?*

- *Is there someone who is experiencing great joy? How could you join with him or her in thanking God for his blessings?*

# Talking It Out

Since Christians grow in community, not just in solitude, here are some questions you may want to discuss with another person or in a group. Each "Talking It Out" section is designed with this purpose in mind.

1. Do you set aside certain times of the day to spend in prayer, or do you "make your life a prayer" (1 Thessalonians 5:17) as you go about your daily activities? Or perhaps both?

2. What do the topics of your current prayer life reveal about your relationship with God?

3. What is the tone of your current prayer life? Is it rich and full of meaning? Is it distracted and unfocused? What would you say about it?

4. What would your ideal prayer life look like? What steps could you take to reach that ideal?

5. When you receive an answer to prayer, do you take the time to praise the Lord for his blessings? For what recent blessing are you the most thankful?

6. How do you think a study of the book of Psalms will influence and enhance your prayer life and your relationship with God?

# LESSON 2

# Joy in God's Character

## (Psalm 111)

I see the wrong that round me lies,
I feel the guilt within;
I hear, with groan and travail-cries,
The world confess its sin.
Yet, in the maddening maze of things,
And tossed by storm and flood,
To one fixed trust my spirit clings;
I know that God is good!

—JOHN GREENLEAF WHITTIER, "THE ETERNAL GOODNESS"

*Additional psalms focused on the character of God: 99, 100*

The great evangelist Dwight L. Moody was once asked how he maintained his relationship with God through the many challenges and difficulties that he faced in his ministry. Here is his reply:

I have come to Him as the best friend I
have ever found, and I can trust Him in that
relationship. I have believed He is Savior; I
have believed He is God; I have believed His

atonement on the cross is mine, and I have come to Him and submitted myself on my knees, surrendered everything to Him, and gotten up and stood by His side as my friend and there isn't any problem in my life, there isn't any uncertainty in my work but I turn and speak to Him as naturally as to someone in the same room, and I have done it these years because I can trust Jesus.[6]

God is good, God is trustworthy, God is faithful and true. His character should birth within us a deep and abiding sense of joy. Let's praise him for it!

## Joy, Despite Our Circumstances

James Guthrie was a Scottish minister who went to the scaffold in 1661 because of his faith in Christ. In telling his story, Jock Purves writes: "James Guthrie ever kept through his busy life his own personal fellowship with Christ in the fresh joyous bloom of his new birth, as if he had been but a young convert." Waking about 4:00 a.m. on the day he was to be executed, Guthrie spent time in personal worship and soon was asked by his friend, James Cowie, how he felt. "Very well," Guthrie replied. Then he quoted Psalm 118:24: "'This is the day that the Lord has made; let us rejoice and be glad in it!'"[7]

God has given us the book of Psalms not only to teach us how to pray and praise and worship him but also to show us how we can have joy in our lives no matter what we are going through. As we read the words of the psalmist—including David in some of his darkest moments—they teach us that joy is not based on our outward circumstances. That's happiness. Joy and happiness are not the same. You can be happy when you win the lottery, but you can have joy even when your bank account is overdrawn and the bills are piling up. You can be happy when you get a promotion at work; you can have joy even when the economy tanks and you are laid off from your job. How is this possible? The book of Psalms teaches us that we can tap into the joy of the Lord at any time because we know the character of our God and that he is trustworthy and good. As Romans 8:28 states so clearly: "We are convinced that every detail of our lives is continually woven together for good, for we are his lovers who have been called to fulfill his designed purpose."

- *Tell of a time when God "wove" the bad circumstances in your life into something good.*

- *Tell of a time when the circumstances stayed bad, but your sense of joy remained. How was this possible for you?*

# He Is Worthy to Be Praised

Let's take a look at God's character in the Psalms and find reasons to have joy—no matter what!

## God Is Mysterious

> God's mighty miracles astound me!
> His wonders are so delightfully mysterious
> that they leave all who seek them astonished.
> (Psalm 111:2)

God and his ways are not mysterious in a spooky or frightening way. Rather, they are "delightfully mysterious." His thoughts, his actions, and even his attributes are beyond us. We can know some truths about him and how he works, but because he is unlimited and we are not, mystery will still surround him no matter how much we get to know him.

• *In what ways do God's nature and goodness surprise you?*

## God Is Perfect

Everything he does is full of splendor and
beauty!
Each miracle demonstrates his eternal
perfection. (v. 3)

God's perfection extends to everything that he does.

• *How have you seen God's perfection exhibited in the
works he has performed in your life?*

## God Is Gracious and Merciful

His unforgettable works of surpassing wonder
reveal his grace and tender mercy. (v. 4)

God's grace and mercy ensure that we do not receive what we
deserve, but instead we are given an overflow of his goodness
and love.

- *Describe a time when God was gracious to you despite what you really deserved. Then thank him for his mercy and grace in your life.*

## God Is Trustworthy

> He satisfies all who love and trust him,
> and he keeps every promise he makes. (v. 5)

As human beings, we all make and break promises—none of us is entirely trustworthy. But God "keeps every promise he makes."

- *How has God proved himself trustworthy to you in the past?*

- *In what areas do you need to trust God more?*

- *How can remembering the promises he has already kept help you to trust him now?*

## God Is Powerful

> He reveals mighty power and marvels to his
> people. (v. 6)

- *Has God revealed his mighty power to you? In what
  ways? What marvels has he performed that you cannot
  help but share?*

## God Is True and Fair

> All God accomplishes is flawless, faithful, and
> fair,
> and his every word proves trustworthy and true.
> They are steadfast forever and ever,
> formed from truth and righteousness. (vv. 7–8)

Truth. Righteousness. Fairness. Faithfulness. These are characteristics that seem rather scarce in our world. But these are the
standards God holds and what he sets for us.

- *How would a healthy dose of these traits change the most troubling situation you are facing right now?*

# WORD WEALTH

God's loving-kindness, his "forever-love," is expressed in the Hebrew word *hesed*.[8] This word is used several times in Exodus 34:6–7: "The Lord, the Lord, the compassionate and gracious God, slow to anger, abounding in love and faithfulness, maintaining love to thousands, and forgiving wickedness, rebellion and sin" (NIV). Divine love and forgiveness go together. God's love forgives; his forgiveness is an expression of his love. *Hesed* is also used in Psalm 111:9:

> [God's] forever-love [*hesed*] paid a full ransom
> for his people
> so that now we're free to come before Yahweh
> to worship his holy and awesome name!

- *How does this verse foreshadow the work Jesus did on the cross? How does this work demonstrate the hesed love of God?*

# ☻ EXPERIENCE GOD'S HEART

Adam and Eve walked with God face-to-face in the garden of Eden. Talking with God was as natural for them as breathing, and they had no fear in the presence of his holiness. But when sin entered the world, everything changed. A holy God could not remain in the presence of sinful people. But he also would not stand to be separated from us forever. So he told Satan, the tempter, in Genesis 3:15 that "great hostility" would exist between Satan and Eve's "seed," who was ultimately Jesus Christ, and that her seed would fatally crush Satan while he would wound Jesus but not fatally. The victory would go to God's Son, Jesus, who we know from later revelation would ransom himself as payment for our sins (Romans 3:21–26; Ephesians 2:1–7; Colossians 2:14–15). Now we can freely come before God to worship him and serve him in spirit and in truth (John 4:22–24).

- *Write a prayer thanking God for what Jesus did for you on the cross, which now allows you to freely approach the Father. Make this a psalm from your heart to his.*

- *The next time you face a difficult challenge in your life, make the active decision to be joyful anyway. Try putting on some praise music and spend time worshiping the Lord. Take note of how your attitude and disposition change as you spend time in his presence.*

# ♥ SHARE GOD'S HEART

*Decision* magazine tells the story of two friends, Gavin and Chuck, who helped out in the teen ministry of their church. Chuck tells what happened during one youth event:

> Gavin and I were helping my pastor guide thirty lively teens through an all-night "lock-in" at church. Early in the evening, Gavin challenged me to a game of table tennis in the fellowship hall. Our game quickly heated up.
>
> With the score tied and only three points to go before the end of the game, Tracy, an eighth grader, grabbed the ball and kept it from us. My first impulse was irritation. But then a Scripture passage that our group had read that afternoon came to mind: "Love is patient, love is kind. It does not envy, it does not boast, it is not proud. It is not rude, it is not self-seeking, it is not easily angered, it keeps no record of wrongs."
>
> Gavin and I joked with Tracy until she finally tossed the ball back onto the table. We thanked her and finished the game.
>
> Hours later, after an evangelistic film, Tracy walked down the aisle with six others to receive Christ as Savior. Later that night, when we gathered for testimonies, Tracy said, "I grew up in a family where nobody goes to church. I've learned to get attention by making people mad at me. But earlier this evening I saw something different."

Gavin and I looked at each other and raised our eyebrows. "When I stole the ball from those guys," she said, pointing at us, "they didn't get mad at me. They didn't fight back. I decided right then that I wanted whatever it was they have."[9]

Many people who don't believe in God are put off by the bad behavior of those whom they see in the church or who call themselves Christians but do not truly follow Jesus and his ways. We are called to be like Christ, and he is the "dazzling radiance of God's splendor, the exact expression of God's true nature—his mirror image!" (Hebrews 1:3).

- *Which characteristics of God that are described in this psalm do you think Christians most need to live out in front of an unbelieving world?*

- *As Christians demonstrate the love, goodness, trustworthiness, and mercy of God, how could they then change our witness for Christ on the earth?*

- *Which characteristics could you develop more in your own life, and how would that make you a more effective witness for Jesus to the people around you?*

# Talking It Out

1. Which of the characteristics of God described in this lesson most resonates with you?

2. Which divine traits do you most need to see demonstrated in yourself or in others? Why?

3. Why is a prayer to God describing his characteristics so important? Does God need a reminder of who he is and what he does? Or does the one who offers the prayer need reminding? Explain your answer.

4. What constitutes "passionate praise" (Psalm 111:1)? How can you include more passion in your prayer life and your worship of God?

# LESSON 3

# Joy in God's Creation

## (Psalms 8, 104, 148)

You, our Creator, formed the earth,
and you hold it all together so it will never fall apart.

—Psalm 104:5

*Additional psalms of creation: 19, 29, 33*

If we possessed an atlas of our galaxy that
devoted but a single page to each star system
in the Milky Way (so that the sun and all its
planets were crammed in one page), that atlas
would run to more than ten million volumes of
ten thousand pages each. It would take a library
the size of Harvard's to house the atlas, and
merely to flip through it, at the rate of a page
per second, would require over ten thousand
years...And there are a hundred billion more
galaxies.[10]

Our God is an amazing God—the Creator of our entire world
and everything in it, including countless galaxies beyond ours.

Psalm 8—among other psalms—is a song of praise to the Creator, showcasing his splendor throughout his creation. As the psalmist stands in the presence of such a powerful and glorious God, he wonders: "Why would you bother with puny, mortal man or care about human beings?" (8:4). The joy that God's creation sparks inside of our hearts is difficult to comprehend.

- *Have you ever felt "small" when you considered the vastness of the created world? Perhaps while looking at a night sky filled with stars or when watching ocean waves crash against the shore? What feelings filled your heart? How do these feelings prompt you to worship the God of creation?*

King David certainly felt small when compared to God's creation, yet he recognized that God had created human beings and set them as the highest created beings on the earth, giving them dominion over the world that he had made (vv. 5–8). And the writer of Psalm 104 showcases the compassion that God, the Creator, has for his creation, including you and me.

- *Read Psalm 104:5–21. How does God show his love for his creation? What evidence do we have that he cares for human beings?*

- *How have you seen this love of God demonstrated in your own life?*

#  DIGGING DEEPER

As you read through Psalm 148, take note of how many parts of God's creation the psalmist commands to praise the Lord. From the sun and the moon to the trees, mountains, and hills, everything that God created showcases his glory.

- *How does the majesty of God's creation remind you to praise him?*

- *How can you use the beauty of nature to help you remember not only his power but also his love for you in your day-to-day life?*

- How does this bring a new sense of joy into your circumstances?

- Read Psalm 148:10–12. Who is commanded to praise the Lord? Is anyone excluded? Why or why not?

# So Many "Extras"!

Sherlock Holmes is a fictional character created by the Scottish novelist Arthur Conan Doyle. Sherlock Holmes and his companion, Dr. Watson, solve numerous crimes due to Holmes' keen powers of observation. The writer Doyle used Sherlock Holmes' rationality and deduction skills to make a point about God in the novel *The Adventure of the Naval Treaty*. In the story, Dr. Watson walked into a room to find Holmes deep in study. Holmes was analyzing a flower. Watson described what happened next:

> He walked past the couch to an open window and held up the drooping stalk of a moss rose, looking down at the dainty blend of crimson and green. It was a new phase of his character for me, for I had never before seen him show an interest in natural objects.

> "There is nothing in which deduction is so necessary as in religion," said he, leaning with his back against the shutters... "Our highest assurance of the goodness of Providence seems to me to rest in the flowers. All other things, our powers, our desires, our food, are really necessary for our existence in the first instance. But this rose is an extra. Its smell and its color are an embellishment of life, not a condition of it. It is only goodness which gives extras, and so I say again that we have much to hope for from the flowers."[11]

- *What "extras" do you see in your life for which you can enjoy and thank God today?*

- *How does his creation inspire you to thank him for the "extras" he has provided?*

# EXPERIENCE GOD'S HEART

In his book *Forged by Fire*, Bob Reccord writes about a severe injury he suffered and lessons he learned from the Lord:

> I had a severe cervical spinal injury. The pain was so excruciating that the hospital staff couldn't do an MRI until I was significantly sedated. The MRI showed significant damage at three major points in the cervical area. Because of the swelling of injured nerve bundles, the only way I could relieve the pain was to use a strong, prescribed narcotic and to lie on bags of ice. Sleep, what little there was, came only by sitting in a reclining chair.
>
> Approximately forty-eight hours from the onset of the injury, doctors estimated that I had lost about 80 percent of the strength in my left arm. Three fingers on my left hand totally lost feeling. The slightest movements would send pain waves hurtling down my left side and shoulder. I had to step away completely from my work (which I love) and wear a neck brace twenty-four hours a day for five weeks.
>
> About halfway through that experience, I was sitting on the screened-in porch behind our home. The day was cold and blustery, but I needed a change of scenery. Suddenly a bird landed on the railing and began to sing. On that cold, rainy day, I couldn't believe any creature had a reason to sing. I wanted to shoot that bird! But he

continued to warble, and I had no choice but to listen.

The next day I was on the porch again, but this time it was bright, sunny, and warm. I was tempted to feel sorry for myself when suddenly the bird (at least it looked like the same one) returned. And he was singing again! Where was that shotgun?

Then it hit me: the bird sang in the cold rain as well as the sunny warmth. His song was not altered by outward circumstances, but it was held constant by an internal condition. It was as though God quietly said to me, "You've got the same choice, Bob. You will either let external circumstances mold your attitude, or your attitude will rise above the external circumstances. You choose!"[12]

• *Has nature ever reminded you of the grace and goodness of God? Tell the story.*

- *Read Psalm 19:1–6. Do you have a favorite place outside in the natural world where you like to worship and pray? If so, where is it, and what about it inspires you to praise the Lord? If not, how could you find a location out-of-doors, preferably in nature, to regularly meet with your Creator?*

 THE EXTRA MILE

The next time it is possible, consider taking a nature walk with God. As you encounter various aspects of his creation—a bird flitting across your path, a babbling brook, the tree branches stretching toward the sky—praise him for his care for all of creation—and for his care for you. Enjoy what he has made, including his creation of you.

# ♥ SHARE GOD'S HEART

Some people are able to look around them and acknowledge God's amazing creation. Others have difficulty seeing past the pressures and stresses of daily life to notice the beauty of nature and the love letter it is from their Creator. Elizabeth Barrett Browning once wrote:

> Earth's crammed with heaven,
> And every common bush afire with God;
> But only he who sees takes off his shoes—
> The rest sit round it and pluck blackberries.[13]

- *Who in your life needs to be reminded today of the Creator's love for them? How might you help them to remember? (Consider ideas that bring the beauty of nature to them: perhaps give them a small bouquet of wildflowers or a potted plant or invite them on a walk through a park on your lunch break.)*

# Talking It Out

1. In our secular society, many people take the theory of naturalistic evolution as fact, believing that the entire world we see and the galaxies beyond were formed by physical processes and mere chance. How do the writers of the book of Psalms contradict this view?

2. Psalm 8 refers to all of creation and "every living thing" as being placed "in submission to Adam's sons" (vv. 7–8). What does this mean for us as stewards of the world around us? What is our responsibility while tending to the earth?

3. Psalm 19:1–4 reminds us that the entire world sees how God is revealed in what he has made. Theologians refer to this as general revelation—what God has shown about himself in the natural world. This revelation is available to everyone, and the apostle Paul refers to the truth it conveys when he says that God has made visible "from the creation of the world, the invisible qualities of God's nature...such as his eternal power and transcendence" (Romans 1:20). How does the fact of general revelation help you more fully connect with God? Also, how can you use it to direct others to see some of the evidence of God in the natural universe?

## LESSON 4

# Joy in God's Coming Messiah

### (Psalm 22)

Christ is the central figure in biblical revelation.

—Dan DeHaan

*Additional messianic psalms: 2:1–12; 16:1–11; 31:1–24;
40:1–17; 41:9–13; 45:6–7; 69:7–21; 72:1–19; 110:1–6;
118:1–29*

It has been said that Jesus can be found in every book of the Bible, from the seed of the woman (Genesis 3:15) to Isaiah's Suffering Servant and Prince of Peace (Isaiah 9; 53). The gospel of Jesus, the Messiah, is also intricately woven throughout the book of Psalms. In Luke 24:44, Jesus told two of his followers: "Don't you remember the words that I spoke to you when I was still with you? I told you that I would fulfill everything written about me, including all the prophecies from the law of Moses through the Psalms and the writings of the prophets." Many of these prophecies are found in the messianic psalms—prophecies that pointed to our Redeemer and Savior many hundreds of years before he walked on the earth in human flesh. These particular psalms all foretold Jesus' nature, work, betrayal, suffering, death, and resurrection.

# 🅝 WORD WEALTH

The messianic psalms speak of Jesus, the coming Messiah, the one whose coming the Jews awaited. The word *messiah* is the Hebrew word for the Greek word *Christ*; both mean "the anointed one." According to Bible scholar Lawrence Richards, *messiah* is "used primarily in the books of 1 and 2 Samuel and Psalms to designate Israel's king. In Psalms it is often a poetic synonym for the royal office. Particularly, it is used to identify the royal line of David (Ps 2:2; 18:50; 84:9; 89:38, 51; 132:10, 17)." Moreover, "it is evident in the OT [Old Testament] that a ruler from David's line will come and will establish an eternal kingdom (e.g., Isa 9:7; 11:1–5)." In the New Testament, "Jesus is identified as the ultimate Anointed One, the one who will rule as king over a restored Davidic kingdom. This conviction is expressed in Jesus' title 'Christ.' This is not a name but a title that means 'the anointed.'"[14]

# 🅒 DIGGING DEEPER

Let's take a closer look at specific references to the future Messiah, Jesus Christ, that can be found in the Psalms—along with their corresponding fulfillment in the New Testament.

- Look up each of the following verses and write out which aspects of Jesus' life, death, and resurrection they describe.

  *Psalm 2:7; Hebrews 1:5*

*Psalm 40:7–8; Hebrews 10:7*


*Psalm 118:22; Matthew 21:42*


*Psalm 41:9; Luke 22:47*


*Psalm 35:11; Luke 23:10–13*


*Psalm 69:21; Matthew 27:34*

*Psalm 22:16; John 20:25*

*Psalm 22:8; Matthew 27:43*

*Psalm 22:1; Matthew 27:46; Mark 15:34*

*Psalm 22:31; John 19:30*

*Psalm 16:8–10; Acts 2:29–31; 13:35–37*

# Psalm 22: What Jesus Did for Us

In Psalm 22 alone, there are thirty-three individual prophecies that relate to Jesus' death on the cross.

- *Read through this psalm. How many prophecies can you identify?*

- *What stands out to you the most in this graphic portrayal of Jesus' suffering?*

# ❦ EXPERIENCE GOD'S HEART

Give me back my life.
Save me from this violent death.
Save my precious one and only
from the power of these dogs!
—Psalm 22:20

Regarding the phrase "Save my precious one and only," Brian Simmons notes that "precious" can also be translated "unique" or "darling." He then goes on to say: "Each of us is that 'one and only' child or 'unique darling'...See Song. 6:9. On the cross, Jesus—like a deer giving birth at the dawning light (see inscription of Ps. 22)—cared less that his body was being torn apart and more about our protection and salvation. He prayed for us as he faced death on the cross."[15]

- The realization that Jesus was thinking of you as his "unique darling" while he was suffering on the cross can be life changing. How might this understanding of how much he loves you bring more joy

  *In your daily walk with him?*

*In your prayer life?*




*In your praise and worship?*




- *Read Psalm 2—The Coronation of the King—which refers to Jesus' royal status as God's Son. Then write a prayer of thanks and praise to God for the work he did for your salvation.*

# ❤ SHARE GOD'S HEART

The Jewish people are still looking for the first coming of the Messiah. Despite the many Old Testament prophecies that Jesus' life, death, and resurrection fulfilled, they still believe that he was just a "good man."

- *Besides the verses we have studied here in the messianic psalms, what other Old Testament passages do you know of that look forward to the life and work of Jesus?*

- *What would you say to a Jew today who doesn't believe that Jesus is the Messiah?*

In his *Encyclopedia of Biblical Prophecy*, Bible scholar J. Barton Payne states that there are 127 distinct predictions concerning the first and second comings of Jesus Christ, and they are set forth in 3,348 verses. More than a hundred of those prophecies apply to Jesus' first coming.[16] In his book *The New Evidence That Demands a Verdict*, apologist Josh McDowell mentions the work of the mathematician Peter Stoner concerning just eight of these prophecies being fulfilled in the life of a single individual:

> We might find that the chance that any man might have lived down to the present time and fulfilled all eight prophecies is one in ten (to the seventeenth power). That would be one in 100,000,000,000,000,000. In order to help us comprehend this staggering probability, Stoner illustrates it by supposing that we take ten (to the seventeenth power) silver dollars and lay them on the face of Texas. They will cover all of the state two feet deep. Now mark one of these silver dollars and stir the whole mass thoroughly, all over the state. Blindfold a man and tell him that he can travel as far as he wishes, but he must pick up one silver dollar and say that "This is the right one." What chance would he have of getting the right one? Just the same chance that the prophets would have had of writing these eight prophecies and having them all come true in any one man.[17]

- *How could arming yourself with this knowledge better equip you to share the gospel with those who don't believe?*

# Talking It Out

1. Consider these other references to Jesus in the book of Psalms. What do they say about him?

    1. *2:1–12*

*2. 31:1–24*

*3. 45:6–7*

*4. 72:1–19*

*5. 110:1–6*

2. Read through the account of Jesus' passion in the Gospel of John (see especially John 19). How does this reading inform your understanding and appreciation for the words of Psalm 22?

3. The first twenty-one verses of Psalm 22 describe the psalmist's experience of extreme suffering and anguish, to the point that it foreshadows Jesus' ultimate suffering and death on the cross. But in verse 22, the psalmist turns a sharp corner from pouring out his troubles to God to praising him for his goodness and love. What made the difference in the psalmist's attitude? How can you continue to praise and worship God in times of great pain and anguish? How can you have joy no matter what happens in your life?

# LESSON 5

# Joy in God's Salvation

## (Psalm 103)

*For the Lord alone is my Savior.*
*What a feast of favor and bliss he gives his people!*

—PSALM 3:8

*Additional psalm concerning God's salvation: 3*

The Bible tells us all about the salvation that God offers to each of us. The Old Testament looks forward to the coming of Jesus Christ, the one who would bring salvation to the world. The New Testament shares the story of Jesus' life, death, and resurrection as well as teaches us about the doctrine of salvation—how we can be saved and what that really means for our lives here and now and for our lives after the grave.

Rather than delving further into the *doctrine* of salvation, however, the poetic prayers of praise found in Psalm 103 convey what the *experience* of our salvation is really like. And how could these words bring anything but joy to our hearts?

- As you read Psalm 103, consider the following aspects of God's salvation. In verses 3–5, King David describes five specific ways in which God saved him—and us! Read them here:

> You kissed my heart with forgiveness, in spite of all I've
> done.
> You've healed me inside and out from every disease.
> You've rescued me from hell and saved my life.
> You've crowned me with love and mercy.
> You satisfy my every desire with good things.

- *To which of these five actions of God can you most relate
  right now? Why?*

- *Which of these do you need to perform in your life today?
  Explain.*

- *How can these reminders of God's work in David's life help you to trust God for what you need in your own life today?*

- *What other "miracles of kindness" (v. 2) has God performed in your life?*

# God's Great Forgiveness

- Read Psalm 103:8–14 and consider the many comparisons David makes to describe the compassion and forgiveness of God.

    *Which of these means the most to you?*

    *Which of these helps to expand your understanding of how much God loves you?*

 WORD WEALTH

The Hebrew word *yatsar* can be translated "form" or "frame." God knows our frame. But *yatsar* also has a homonym that means "to be in distress" or "to be frustrated." So this sentence could be translated "You know all about our frustrations and distress." These thoughts combined would mean that God hasn't forgotten that he formed us from dust and we'll experience frustrations as human beings. God is sympathetic to our difficulties.[18]

To be human in this fallen world means that we will experience distress, disappointment, and frustration. While that may sound like bad news, David was actually sharing *good news* in this psalm—the fact that *God understands*! We don't have to try to hide our challenges and frustrations from him. He already knows "all about us, inside and out" (v. 14). And he stands ready to help. Because of his love, mercy, and compassion, our peace and joy can remain steadfast no matter what struggles we experience.

- *For some people, deep levels of intimacy with another bring feelings of distress or anxiety. Why do you suppose that is? What thoughts and emotions does the truth that God knows everything about you—inside and out—bring up for you?*

- *What distress or frustrations are you experiencing today? Bring them to the Lord—he understands.*

# ◐ EXPERIENCE GOD'S HEART

Ultimately, Psalm 103 is a psalm of praise—which is the correct response when we truly realize how great our salvation is. David's conclusion is a crescendo of blessing, praise, and worship to the Lord. Just take a look at the joy that he expresses in these words:

> So bless the Lord, all his messengers of power,
> for you are his mighty heroes who listen intently
> to the voice of his word to do it.
> Bless and praise the Lord, you mighty warriors,
> ministers who serve him well and fulfill his
> desires.
> I will bless and praise the Lord with my whole
> heart!
> Let all his works throughout the earth,
> wherever his dominion stretches—
> let everything bless the Lord!
> —Psalm 103:20–22

- *Consider the various groups of worshipers in these verses (God's messengers of power; God's mighty heroes who obey his word; the mighty warriors of the Lord; ministers who serve him well). With which group do you most identify? Why would you choose this group?*

- *Verses 1 and 22 of Psalm 103 are the opening and closing stanzas of this psalm of praise. Read them aloud as an offering of your worship to the Lord.*

- *What would it mean to bow with your "whole life" before God? How can you do this in practical ways today?*

# ♥ SHARE GOD'S HEART

Psalm 103:15–16 speaks to the brevity of life. We never know how long we may have to share with others the love of God and his offer of salvation for all humankind.

> Dwight L. Moody made a mistake on October 8, 1871. He preached to his largest audience in the city of Chicago. The text had been, "What Will You Do Then with Jesus Who Is Called the Christ?" He said something he had never said before and, frankly, never said again. He was very fatigued and because of that he said to the audience after he presented the gospel, "Now I will give you a week to think that over. And when we come together again, you will have the opportunity to respond."
>
> Then Ira Sankey came and began to sing. Even before he finished the song, you could hear the blare of the siren in the streets of Chicago as that great fire broke out and left 100,000 homeless. Hundreds of people died in that fire. And Dwight L. Moody rose to the occasion a few months later and said, "I would give my right arm before I would ever give an audience another week to think over the message of the gospel. Some who heard that night died in the fire."[19]

The Bible tells us that "Now is the time to respond to [God's] favor! Now is the day of salvation!" (2 Corinthians 6:2).

---

- *Who needs to hear from you today about God's great offer of salvation? How can you share his love in a meaningful way with them—without procrastinating?*

# Talking It Out

1. When human beings "forgive" one another, it often looks a lot different from the way that God forgives. Psalm 103:9–10 gives us insight into how God forgives. How does it differ from human forgiveness? How does God's way of forgiving inspire you to forgive the people in your life who have offended you?

2. What truths about God's salvation bring you the most joy?

3. If you are in a group setting, try the fun exercise of writing your own psalm together. Take turns contributing a line or a stanza, praising and thanking God for the various ways in which he has saved each of you.

## LESSON 6

# Joy in God's Forgiveness

## (Psalm 51)

God paints in many colors; but He never paints so gorgeously...
as when He paints in white.

—G. K. CHESTERTON

*Additional psalms concerning God's forgiveness: 65, 85*

John Alexander wrote these words years ago in his publication *The Other Side*: "Sin is the best news there is, because with sin, there's a way out. You can't repent of confusion or psychological flaws inflicted by your parents—you're stuck with them. But you can repent of sin. Sin and repentance are the only grounds for hope and joy, the grounds for reconciled, joyful relationships."[20]

- *Do you agree with the statement, "Sin is the best news there is"? Why or why not?*

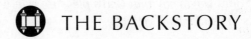

# THE BACKSTORY

Psalm 51 is a psalm of repentance written by King David after his sin with Bathsheba.

- *Read 2 Samuel 11–13. Briefly recount what David did and the fallout of his actions.*

- *Now return to Psalm 51 and read it while keeping in mind David's sin and its consequences. What do you learn from this psalm of confession about David's repentance and plea to God?*

- *What does David say that God's pleasure is in when it comes to us (51:16–17)?*

# Sin Separates Us from God

According to Psalm 8, God created people as good, just a little lower than the angels, "crowned with glory and magnificence" (v. 5). Psalm 51, however, shows that all human beings—even King David himself—commit sin, falling short of God's righteous standards (see Romans 3:23).

- *Sin is a word used less and less in our culture. Why do you think that is?*

- *What words or phrases do we tend to use instead of "sin" to soften the word's impact? (For example, someone "told a white lie.")*

- *Do you think that calling sin "sin" would make a difference in how we respond to it? Explain your answer.*

There are many consequences to sin, but the greatest is that it separates us from God. His holiness cannot remain in the presence of our unholiness.

• *What did David ask God to do about his sin?*

• *What was the result?*

# EXPERIENCE GOD'S HEART

A key passage from this psalm—and in the whole of Scripture—is Psalm 51:10–11:

> Keep creating in me a clean heart.
> Fill me with pure thoughts and holy desires,
> ready to please you.
> May you never reject me!
> May you never take from me your sacred Spirit!

As the translator writes in the notes for these verses: "The word used for 'create' takes us back to Gen. 1, and it means to create from nothing. David knew he had no goodness without God placing it within him. David wanted a new creation heart, not just the old one changed."[21]

- *Psalm 51:10 is the central verse in this psalm, both literally (it is in the exact center of the psalm) and figuratively (its message is the central theme). Write this verse out in your own words, making it a prayer from your own heart to the Lord.*

- *Note the change in David's attitude from before the key verses 10–11 to after he prays these words to the Lord. How can our repentance of sin lead to the type of restoration of our relationship with God that David experienced in verses 14–19?*

- *How have you experienced God's forgiveness in your own life? Did it cause you to rejoice as David did? Tell the story, including as many details as you feel comfortable sharing.*

- *What truths about God's forgiveness bring you the most joy?*

 SHARE GOD'S HEART

Let my passion for life be restored,
tasting joy in every breakthrough you bring to
me.
Hold me close to you with a willing spirit
that obeys whatever you say.
Then I can show other guilty ones
how loving and merciful you are.
They will find their way back home to you,
knowing that you will forgive them.
—Psalm 51:12–13

- *Who in your life needs to experience the love and mercy of God today?*

- *How can you help that person "find their way back home"?*

# Talking It Out

1. David states very clearly that he has been a "sinner from birth" (v. 5). Sin, therefore, is something more than just committing a bad act. What does David mean? Pay special attention to what else David says in Psalm 51 about where he finds sin within him and what needs to be done in him to address it.

2. Despite David's prayer of repentance, he still faced the consequences of his sin (read 2 Samuel 12:13–23). Was this fair or unfair? Explain your answer.

3. The commentary on Psalm 51:9 says this: "David was ashamed not just of what others would think but also that he had been seen by God. A truly remorseful person has no thought for reputation but only for righteousness."[22] How can you identify a "truly remorseful person"?

# LESSON 7

# Joy in God's Protection

## (Psalm 91)

Plagues and deaths around me fly;
Till he bids, I cannot die.

—Anonymous

*Additional psalms concerning God's protection: 59, 61*

Many years ago, the newspaper columnist Eppie Lederer, more famously known as Ann Landers, would answer the questions of people who wrote to share with her their problems and ask her for advice on a wide variety of issues. During the peak of her success, she received, on average, over ten thousand letters each month. At one point, she was asked if there was "one underlying predominant theme" in the letters she received. "The one problem above all others," she said, "seems to be fear. People are afraid of losing their health, their wealth, and their loved ones. People are afraid of life itself."[23]

- *What are your fears? Among them, what do you fear losing more than anything else?*

# "Don't Fear a Thing!"

- *Read through Psalm 91. What specific fears do you have that this section of Scripture addresses?*

• *When the psalmist writes, "Don't fear a thing!" in verse 6, that essentially encompasses any danger or concern we might ever face in our lives. What specific fears do you have that this psalm does not mention?*

• *How can you trust in God's protection for anything that concerns you?*

# Angels Watching over Me

There is a once-popular song by Amy Grant in which she sings about the many near-misses and averted tragedies we may never know about because of God's angels watching over us and protecting us. The song has its basis in Psalm 91:11–12—and its message is true. We have unseen guardians who go before us and behind us, guiding us and protecting us, and we are rarely even aware of their presence. Billy Graham once said this about the angels that God assigns to each of us:

> One of the most comforting truths in all the Bible to me as I travel from one part of the world to another is to know that God has stationed His heavenly guards to protect, guide, and lead me through life's dangerous way. I cannot see these beings with my physical eyes, but I sense they are present every day.[24]

- *Have you ever had an experience in which you had a sense that God was protecting you? Briefly tell about it here.*

- *Now write a prayer of praise, thanking God for his angels who guard and protect you in everything that you do.*

# DIGGING DEEPER

Theologian C. Fred Dickason provides a brief overview of the protective role that angels play as spelled out in Scripture:

> Angels minister to God by protecting His people...They may harass our enemies (Ps 35:4–5) and deliver us from their wicked works (Ps 34:7; Is 63:9). They are probably involved in physically preserving God's own for their future inheritance in His presence and kingdom (Heb 1:14).
>
> ...Angels often guard God's people and keep them from physical danger. Jacob may have had the protection of angels as he traveled with his family to meet Esau (Gen 32:1–32). Daniel knew that God had

sent His angel to shut the lions' mouths, an evidence of Daniels' innocency and of God's power and faithfulness (Dan 6:20–23). The three Hebrew youths seem to have had an angel keeping them from harm in the fiery furnace (Dan 3:24–28).

When Israel's king sent an army to capture Elisha at Dothan, the prophet told his fearful servant, "Fear not: for they that be with us are more than they that be with them" (2 Ki 6:16, cf. vv. 13–17). He then prayed, and God revealed an angelic army surrounding and protecting God's men.[25]

While all of us experience injustice and harm at times in our lives, one day in heaven we will learn how many times angels protected and preserved us. God cares for his people.

# 🄷 WORD WEALTH

The word *Shaddai* used in the first verse of Psalm 91 has many different meanings,[26] but all of them should inspire praise to the Lord for his loving protection, shelter, and care.

- Consider each of these descriptions of the Lord. Which resonates with you the most? Why?

*God of the Mountain:*

*God the Destroyer of Enemies:*

*God the Self-Sufficient One:*

*God the Nurturer of Babies:*

*God the Almighty:*

• *What influence do these truths about God have on your joy?*

# A Two-Way Street

Here is what the Lord has spoken to me:
"Because you loved me, delighted in me, and
have been loyal to my name,
I will greatly protect you.
I will answer your cry for help every time you
pray,
and you will feel my presence
in your time of trouble.
I will deliver you and bring you honor.
I will satisfy you with a full life and with all that
I do for you.
For you will enjoy the fullness of my salvation!"
—Psalm 91:14–16

God protects those whom he loves and those who love him in
return.

• *What are the "because...then" statements found within
these verses?*

- *What happens "every time" we pray?*




- *How do these promises from the Lord prompt you to thank and praise him?*

 EXPERIENCE GOD'S HEART

- Read again the incredible promise found in Psalm 91:14. In what ways do you love God and delight in him? How do you express your love for him and delight in him in the following areas of your life?

*Your habits:*

*Your work life:*

*Your finances:*

*Your family:*


*Your other relationships:*


*Your ministry:*


• *What truths about God's protection bring you the most joy?*

# ❤ SHARE GOD'S HEART

- *How can praising God in the midst of challenging and difficult times be a witness to others who need to know of his loving care?*

# Talking It Out

1. If someone continues to experience problems in life after becoming a Christ-follower—if they are diagnosed with a terminal illness, file for bankruptcy, are served with divorce papers, or otherwise seem not to receive the benefits promised in Psalm 91—does that mean that God did not hear that person's prayers? Why or why not? Why should we praise God anyway, even when bad things happen?

2. If God is truly our stronghold (v. 2), our shield (v. 4), our hiding place (v. 9), and our protector (v. 14), how might these truths lead us to react differently to the circumstances of life? How would these responses differ from the "normal" reaction of those who might not know the Lord?

3. In what practical ways can you demonstrate your trust in the Lord's protection, not just individually but also in community with other believers?

4. What is the relationship between preparing for challenges and disasters and trusting in God to keep us safe? (For example, some Christians see the purchase of an insurance policy as a sign that a person doesn't trust in God. Or, in an extreme, someone might not see a doctor to treat an illness because they believe God will supernaturally heal them.) What is the balance between the two?

# LESSON 8

# Joy in the Lord, Our Shepherd

## (Psalm 23)

Yahweh is my best friend and my shepherd.
I always have more than enough.
He offers a resting place for me in his luxurious love.
His tracks take me to an oasis of peace
near the quiet brook of bliss.

—Psalm 23:1–2

*Additional psalm concerning God's shepherding care: 29*

Without a doubt, Psalm 23 is the most well-known and beloved of all the psalms. In this beautiful piece of prayer-poetry, David, the shepherd boy, sings his praise to the Lord, whom he sees as *his* very own Shepherd. God provides for David's every need—food, drink, protection and safety, a place to rest, even "luxurious love" and an unfailing hope for the future.

- *What has been your experience with the Twenty-Third Psalm? Did you memorize it as a child in Sunday school? Hear it recited at the funeral of a loved one? Pray it yourself as a reminder of God's care during a particularly troubling time in your life? Tell the story.*

 # THE BACKSTORY

Most scholars believe that David wrote this psalm as a young boy while working in the fields as a shepherd, watching over the flocks of his father, Jesse. (Read 1 Samuel 16 to better understand David's background.) The beautiful piece of poetry David has given us in Psalm 23 describes his relationship with God even before he slayed the giant Goliath, before he was anointed as king, before any of his great exploits occurred. Later in David's life, the Bible describes him as a "man who always pursues [God's] heart" (Acts 13:22). The relationship David cultivated with God as a young shepherd boy, unknown to the world, gave him the spiritual foundation he needed to later fulfill God's great purpose for his life.

- *In what ways are you currently cultivating your relationship with God?*

- *How might the lessons God has been teaching you recently prepare you for his future plans and purpose for your life and ministry?*

# David's Poetic Praise to God

Most of us have heard, recited, or memorized Psalm 23 at some point in our lives—but not in the same language and phrasing as that of The Passion Translation.

- *Read through the psalm in The Passion Translation again. Which newly translated phrase of previously familiar words most stands out to you?*

- *What makes those words so meaningful?*

As the translator of The Passion Translation notes: "The word most commonly used for 'shepherd' is taken from the root word *ra'ah*, which is also the Hebrew word for 'best friend.' This translation includes both meanings."[27]

- *How can the Lord, your Shepherd, also be your best friend?*

- *When you think of a human-to-human, best-friend relationship, what characteristics come to mind?*

- *Do those same characteristics also apply to having God as your best friend? If so, how?*

- *How might friendship with God differ from a friendship with another human being?*

# The Tasks of a Shepherd

Ancient shepherds were tasked with the responsibility of providing everything the sheep in their care could ever need to live a long and healthy life. In David's comparison to the Lord as our Shepherd, God is the Provider of everything we, the "sheep of his pasture," need (Psalm 100:3 NIV).

- God has provided the following for us, his beloved sheep. Read each of these verses and tell how God has provided for each of these needs in your own life.

*Rest (Psalm 23:2):*

*Life (v. 3):*

*Guidance (v. 3):*




*Safety (v. 4):*




*Physical needs (v. 5):*

*Eternal home (v. 6):*

- *How can you show your gratitude and praise the Lord today for the many ways in which he has provided for you?*

# EXPERIENCE GOD'S HEART

> [The Lord] offers a resting place for me in his
> luxurious love.
> His tracks take me to an oasis of peace near the
> quiet brook of bliss.
> That's where he restores and revives my life.
> He opens before me the right path,
> and leads me along in his footsteps of
> righteousness
> so that I can bring honor to his name.
> —Psalm 23:2–3

In the midst of our frenetic, busy modern schedules, we often long for a quiet place to rest. The "resting place," the "oasis of peace," referred to here is a place of soul-deep refreshment. If you have ever had a full night of sleep but woke up still exhausted because of the weight of worry and distraction on your heart, you know the value of restorative time for body, mind, soul, and spirit. Or perhaps you don't sleep much at all—either because you have too much on your plate or too much on your mind. Either way, the Lord, our Shepherd, calls you to come away to a quiet place with him and rest.

• *How can spending quiet, restful time in God's presence restore the joy in our lives?*

- *Do you have a quiet place where you can get away with God and experience the refreshing and reviving replenishment of his Spirit? If so, where is it, and how often do you meet him there? If not, how can you find such a place and work time with God into your schedule?*

 SHARE GOD'S HEART

- *Do you know anyone who needs a reminder of God's shepherding care? Consider writing them a note of encouragement today—either handwritten or by text or email. You might include a few verses of Psalm 23 to strengthen their faith.*

# Talking It Out

1. Psalm 23:4 reads: "Even when your path takes me through the valley of deepest darkness, fear will never conquer me, for you already have! Your authority is my strength and my peace." Psalm 23 doesn't say that our own path could lead us through a "valley of deepest darkness," nor does it say that is the path the enemy might tempt us to take. It says, "Even when *your* path takes me..." Sometimes dark times come—even when we are in the middle of God's will for our lives. Describe a time when you felt in the middle of the "valley of deepest darkness." How did the Lord's joy and peace remain with you in that dark time? How did he lead you through?

2. If we can't have certainty that life will always be easy, what *can* we be certain of? How is this a greater promise than a life of ease and prosperity?

3. Jesus called himself the "Good Shepherd" (read through John 10). Jude 12 also refers to "shepherds" among us, but these shepherds are considered ungodly. What constitutes a "good" shepherd, and how does Jesus fulfill this role for us? How did the shepherds in Jude 12 fail in their task?

4. Bring to memory a time in your life when your heart overflowed (see Psalm 23:5). What did that look like and feel like for you? How can the memories that we have of God's past blessings help us to endure tougher times?

5. Many of the patriarchs—including Abel, Jacob, and Moses—tended to flocks of sheep or herds of other animals, so the metaphor of God as Shepherd would have been familiar to them. Our modern society does not have as many literal shepherds, but we do have other caretaking occupations. How might the love and care of God compare to some of our more modern professions (perhaps a nurse, a teacher, a farmer, a veterinarian, or a day care worker)?

# LESSON 9

# Joy during Times of Waiting

## (Psalm 40)

Don't give up; don't be impatient;
be entwined as one with the Lord.
Be brave and courageous, and never lose hope.
Yes, keep on waiting—for he will never disappoint you!

—PSALM 27:14

*Additional psalm concerning waiting on God: 27*

Red traffic lights.
A long line at the grocery store.
A slow broadband or internet connection.
Traffic jams.
A message from Amazon saying "package delayed."
For some of us, just reading these words can make the blood boil in our veins. Many people would rather do just about anything except wait. But "waiting on the Lord" is different from our usual "hurry up and wait" scenarios in day-to-day life. Waiting on God is never a waste of time; in contrast, it is actually for our benefit—especially when we learn to praise him in expectation of what he will do in and through our lives.

# WORD WEALTH

The Hebrew phrasing used in Psalm 40:1 is an intense expression intended to convey an *active* posture while we are waiting. Literally, it means "While expecting, I expected, expectantly."[28]

- *What is the difference between waiting and expecting?*

- *For what have you waited on the Lord in the past?*

• *What role did expectation play in your time of waiting?*

 THE BACKSTORY

Many scholars believe that David wrote this psalm when he was on the run from King Saul. Saul was jealous of David's exploits, and as he turned away from God later in his life, Saul grew mad with rage and pursued David with murderous intent. Whether or not this was the crisis that David was facing when he wrote this psalm, he certainly was experiencing a time of trouble, and he was waiting for God to move on his behalf.

• First read Psalm 40, and then respond to the following questions.

*Our modern culture places great value on self-sufficiency, on pulling ourselves up "by our bootstraps." Many people believe that given enough money and resources, all of their problems could be solved. But as human beings living in a fallen world, each of us will*

*eventually face "problems greater than [we] can solve"*
*(v. 12). Have you ever faced such a problem? If so, what*
*was your response?*

*What, if anything, could you have done to handle the*
*situation better?*

*How can you trust God more to help you solve problems*
*that are beyond your solving ability?*

# "Just Checking In, Lord!"

Waiting on God is challenging and frustrating to many of us. But God knows that we are human, and he understands our high-speed, modern society, which creates within us the expectation of receiving what we want right now.

- *For what are you waiting on God today? Make a list—as exhaustive as you can—and write out a "check-in" prayer to God, asking him to reveal his will to you in each situation and requesting his assistance in the waiting period.*

- *How tempting is it for you to become impatient in any of these situations?*

- *What is it about that particular request that tries your patience?*




- *How can you praise the Lord right now, regardless of how soon he moves on your behalf?*

# Finding Joy, Even in a "Mess"

Paul Thigpen once shared this account in *Discipleship Journal*:

I remember coming home one afternoon to discover that the kitchen I had worked so hard to clean only a few hours before was now a terrible wreck. My young daughter had obviously been busy "cooking," and the ingredients were scattered, along with dirty bowls and utensils, across the counters and floors. I was not happy with the situation.

Then, as I looked a little more closely at the mess, I spied a tiny note on the table, clumsily written and smeared with chocolatey fingerprints. The message was short—"I'm making sumthin 4 you, Dad"—and it was signed, "Your Angel."

In the midst of that disarray, and despite my irritation, joy suddenly sprang up in my heart, sweet and pure. My attention had been redirected from the problem to the little girl I loved. As I encountered her in that brief note, I delighted in her. With her simple goodness in focus, I could take pleasure in seeing her hand at work in a situation that seemed otherwise disastrous.

The same is true of my joy in the Lord. Many times life looks rather messy; I can't find much to be happy about in my circumstances. Nevertheless, if I look hard enough, I can usually see the Lord behind it all, or at least working through it all, "makin sumthin" for me.[29]

- *How does actively looking for God's hand in your life—in times of waiting or in times of a "mess"—help you tap into the joy of the Lord?*

- *Have you learned to find joy in any situation—good or bad? If not, how can you work on that?*

 EXPERIENCE GOD'S HEART

Each day, we can sing a "new song" to the Lord:

> A new song for a new day rises up in me
> every time I think about how he breaks through
> for me!
> Ecstatic praise pours out of my mouth until
> everyone hears how God has set me free.
> Many will see his miracles;
> they'll stand in awe of God and fall in love with
> him!
> —Psalm 40:3

• *The Lord also tells us that he is doing a new thing in Isaiah 43:19. What "new thing" is God doing for you?*

• *How will this "new thing" change your heart? Your life?*

# 9 SHARE GOD'S HEART

The famous missionary C. T. Studd once traveled to China on a ship whose captain was an embittered opponent of Christianity and who often studied the Bible for the sole reason of arguing with the missionaries who frequently sailed with him. When he learned that C. T. Studd was aboard his ship, the captain lit into him. But instead of arguing with the captain, the missionary put his arm around the man and said, "But, my friend, I have a peace that passes all understanding and a joy that nothing can take away."

The captain finally replied, "You're a lucky dog," and walked away, having nothing left with which to refute the missionary. But apparently Studd's peace and joy were enticing: before the end of the voyage, the captain himself became a rejoicing believer in Jesus![30]

Sharing the amazing deeds that God has done in the past is a great encouragement to others who are going through similar situations, as well as an encouragement to our own hearts. And when God comes through in an incredible way—especially after a long period of waiting—it can cause such excitement that we can't keep it to ourselves! And that excitement could very well draw other people to the Lord.

- *Have you ever experienced such an amazing "miracle" that you couldn't keep it to yourself? Tell the story.*

- *Has anyone ever shared with you an incredible story of what God has done for them? How did it impact your own life and faith?*

- *Read the responses you recorded to the questions above under "Experience God's Heart." Consider sharing your story with a friend over coffee or even on social media. Other people could be blessed by your testimony and even "stand in awe of God and fall in love with him!" (Psalm 40:3).*

# Talking It Out

1. Do you remember being a child and waiting for your birthday or for Christmas to arrive? How did the anticipation of the event enhance the experience for you? Does waiting for God's blessings to arrive inspire the same sense of anticipation in your heart? Why or why not?

2. Who has been a hero in your life? Maybe a parent, a mentor, a coach, or a teacher? Or maybe you are inspired by a fictional superhero who fights evil and stands up for justice. As you read Psalm 40:17, what emotions do you experience as the psalmist calls the Lord his "true Savior and hero"? (The term "hero" is used for God many times in The Passion Translation of the Psalms.) What heroic characteristics does God display in your life?

3. Have you ever greatly anticipated something that turned out to be a huge disappointment? What happened? How might such an experience affect a person's ability to wait on the Lord? What does Psalm 27:14 have to say about this? (Consider memorizing this verse to bolster your faith during times when you are tempted to give up.)

# LESSON 10

# Joy and Thanksgiving

## (Psalms 100 and 107)

If my children wake up on Christmas morning and have
somebody to thank for putting candy in their stockings,
have I no one to thank for putting two feet in mine?

—G. K. CHESTERTON

*Additional psalms concerning offering thanksgiving to God:
18, 30, 32, 92, 118, 138*

Author Brennan Manning once said:

> I believe that the real difference in
> the American church is not between
> conservatives and liberals, fundamentalists
> and charismatics, nor between Republicans
> and Democrats. The real difference is
> between the aware and the unaware.
>     When somebody is aware of that love,
> the same love that the Father has for Jesus,
> that person is just spontaneously grateful.
> Cries of thankfulness become the dominant
> characteristic of the interior life, and the

> byproduct of gratitude is joy. We're not
> joyful and then become grateful—we're
> grateful, and that makes us joyful.[31]

Did you know that the words *think* and *thank* come from the same root—implying that the way we become most thankful is by thinking about everything we have been given and all of the blessings that we enjoy? Psalms 100 and 107 bring these grateful thoughts to the forefront of our minds and help us to share our thankful hearts with the Giver of all good gifts.

In general, the concept of "being thankful" implies having someone to thank. In America, the secular culture kicks off the winter holiday season each year in November with the celebration of Thanksgiving, but simply acknowledging and feeling grateful for one's blessings is a vague and often unfulfilling and meaningless exercise.

- *How does having someone to thank make the blessings you have received more meaningful?*

- *If we are grateful for something, we are less likely to take it for granted. What blessings in your life have you become complacent about?*

- *How can you remind yourself more often of the many blessings you have received?*

# The "Password of Praise"

Worship Yahweh with gladness.
Sing your way into his presence with joy!
And realize what this really means—
we have the privilege of worshiping Yahweh
our God.
For he is our Creator and we belong to him.
We are the people of his pleasure.
You can pass through his open gates with the
password of praise.
Come right into his presence with thanksgiving.
Come bring your thank offering to him
and affectionately bless his beautiful name!
—Psalm 100:2–4

- *Is our praise and worship of God an obligation or a privilege? Or is it both? Explain.*

- *A password is similar to a key—it opens up access to something not typically available. According to Psalm 100, what is the "password" to enter the presence of the Lord?*

- *Why would God welcome into his presence those who come with a spirit of thankfulness? Why is this so pleasing to him?*

# The Importance of Thanksgiving

- *Read through Psalm 107. How many repeated phrases can you find?*

In Hebrew poetry, repetition was a common technique the writers used to place emphasis or importance on certain phrases they wanted their audience to focus on and remember. Zig Ziglar has said, "Repetition is the mother of learning, the father of action, which makes it the architect of accomplishment."[32] Modern scientists agree that repeating information helps us to commit it to memory, but *spaced repetition* (putting some time and/or other information and distractions between the repetitions) really cements the repeated phrases in the mind.[33] Isn't it incredible that this is the very same educational strategy the psalmist used thousands of years ago to teach us the importance of thanksgiving?

## EXPERIENCE GOD'S HEART

We have all heard the phrase "Count your blessings," but not many of us take the time to actually do it. Today, give it a try. On a piece of paper, list the numbers from one to twenty, then next to each number, write a blessing for which you are thankful. Once you reach twenty, why stop there? See how many more blessings you can name. Then spend some time with the Lord, thanking him for everything he has done for you.

## SHARE GOD'S HEART

Make the commitment to do something kind for someone else each day for the next week: for example, let someone in front of you in line, hold a door for someone whose hands are full, compliment a stranger, pay for the food order of the person or family behind you in the drive-thru. Whether or not they thank you in response, be grateful to the Lord for your ability to help and for the kindness he has shown to you in your own life.

# Talking It Out

1. Have you ever done something special for someone—given a costly gift to a loved one, made an extra effort to bless a friend, gone out of your way to help someone in need—and the recipient did not acknowledge your effort, either forgetting or refusing to express their gratitude? How did it make you feel? How might God feel when we forget to thank him for the things he has done for us?

2. What specific things does the psalmist thank God for in Psalms 100 and 107? (See, for example, Psalm 107:8–9.) Why is it important to be specific about what we thank God for? How is this different from praying a general "Thank you for everything" kind of prayer? How does it affect the person who is praying?

3. First Thessalonians 5:18 instructs: "In the midst of everything be always giving thanks, for this is God's perfect plan for you in Christ Jesus." All of us have things in our lives for which we are definitively *not* thankful. How can we resolve this fact with the instruction given in the verse above? Are we to be thankful *for* everything or *in the midst of* everything? What is the difference between the two?

# LESSON 11

# Cultivating Joy Together

## (Psalms 66 and 67)

Many Christians have been infected with the most virulent virus of modern American life, what sociologist Robert Bellah calls "radical individualism." They concentrate on personal obedience to Christ as if all that matters is "Jesus and me," but in doing so miss the point altogether. For Christianity is not a solitary belief system. Any genuine resurgence of Christianity, as history demonstrates, depends on a reawakening and renewal of that which is the essence of the faith—that is, the people of God, the new society, the body of Christ, which is made manifest in the world—the church.[34]

—CHARLES COLSON

*Additional psalms concerning community joyfulness in worship: 63, 124, 129*

"No man is an island," John Milton famously wrote. And he was correct. God created people with the need for, first, a relationship with him and, second, a relationship with other people. Believers, especially, are meant to encourage each other in the Lord.

Praising God in our individual lives is important, for it reminds us of his blessings, and it strengthens our relationship with him.

But the communal worship of the Lord should never be neglected (see Hebrews 10:24–25). Being with other people allows us to praise God together when things are going great in our lives, and it allows us to encourage each other to maintain our joy when things aren't going as well.

- *Read Psalms 66 and 67. What reasons do these psalms give to worship the Lord? (List as many as you can find.)*

- *Why are these reasons for corporate worship and not just for individual worship of God?*

Jesus acknowledged the power of gathering together in prayer and praise when he said, "I give you an eternal truth: If two of you agree to ask God for something in a symphony of prayer, my heavenly Father will do it for you. For wherever two or three come together in honor of my name, I am right there with them!" (Matthew 18:19–20).

- *Do you consistently gather with other believers in a small group setting or in a larger church worship service? With whom do you regularly share the things that God has done in your life?*

## The King of the World

We are not only part of God's church in our local settings. His lordship is not limited to one's city, state, or nation. The Lord is the King of the entire universe!

• *Return to Psalms 66 and 67 and write down the many references to such phrases as "everyone," "all you peoples," "all the people," "all you lovers of God," and "all the nations." According to these references, what are all of us supposed to do?*

Not everyone in the world can worship God freely or without fear of persecution. In fact, more than 360 million Christians—one in seven believers in the world today—experience high levels of persecution, simply for professing their faith in Jesus.[35]

• *What things do all believers have in common worldwide?*

• *How does the realization of these commonalities affect you?*

## EXPERIENCE GOD'S HEART

To the fatherless [God] is a father.
To the widow he is a champion friend.
The lonely he makes part of a family.
The prisoners he leads into prosperity until they
sing for joy.
This is our Holy God in his Holy Place!
—Psalm 68:5–6

You may currently have an earthly father with whom you are at least relatively close. You may still be married, so not a widow. You might not feel lonely at this moment, and you might not literally be in prison. But each of us needs a relationship with our heavenly Father, and each of us longs to be part of a community. None of us wants to be alone, and we have all been bound in the prison of sin and despair. Thankfully, God is the answer for all of these needs!

- *Write a prayer of thanks to God for providing each of these things—and more—for you.*

# SHARING GOD'S HEART

God, keep us near your mercy-fountain and
bless us!
And when you look down on us, may your face
beam with joy!
*Pause in his presence*
Send us out all over the world so that everyone
everywhere
will discover your ways and know who you are
and see your power to save.
—Psalm 67:1–2

As believers in Jesus, each of us is a member of God's worldwide church. Consider ways in which you might support impoverished or persecuted Christians in another part of the world. You might sponsor a child through an organization that provides for both material needs and spiritual needs by sharing the gospel as well as food and clothing. Or create a list of the top countries where it is most costly for believers to follow the Lord and commit to praying for your persecuted brothers and sisters in Christ around the world.[36]

# Talking It Out

1. Have you ever worshiped God in a setting or culture different from your own local church? Perhaps on a mission trip to a different part of the country or to a foreign nation? If so, what was the experience like? How did it differ from what you were used to? What were the similarities? What did you learn from the experience?

2. If you have never been able to attend a worship service like this before, consider visiting a church of a different culture or even a different denomination from your own. (Note: many larger cities have congregations of believers from other nations, cultures, or people groups, such as Latin Americans, South Koreans, or Eastern Europeans.) Then share with another person what the experience was like for you and what you learned about Christ's body, the church.

3. Read Psalm 66:8–12. Why does the psalmist praise God for the fire he passed through and the chains that were placed around his neck? Read Romans 8:28. How are Paul's words similar to the psalmist's song of praise? How has God proven this to be true in your life?

4. As you read the headlines or watch the evening news, you'll soon see that not all nations follow the Lord or submit to his ways. How do the words of Psalm 67:3–7 seem to contradict what we see in our current situation? When might they be fulfilled? (Read Romans 14:10–12 and Philippians 2:10).

## LESSON 12

# Let Everyone Everywhere Joyfully Praise Him!

## (Psalm 150)

Hallelujah! Praise the Lord! Praise God in his holy sanctuary!...
Let everyone everywhere join in the crescendo of ecstatic praise
to Yahweh!
Hallelujah! Praise the Lord!

—PSALM 150:1, 6

*Additional psalms concerning joyfully praising God: 19*

Psalm 150 is the closing chapter of the Bible's book of songs and
prayers. As you read it, consider how fitting it is as the conclusion
of an entire volume of songs to the Lord.

- *Count how many times the word* praise *is used in
  Psalm 150.*

- *It's not possible to say exactly what prompted the psalmist's enthusiastic worship of God, but it's easy to join in. Have you ever been so filled with the joy of the Lord or your amazement at his miraculous works that you had to burst into song? Tell the story.*

## Where Should We Praise God?

- *Verse 1 of Psalm 150 tells us two places where we should joyfully praise the Lord. What are they?*

Those of us still here on the earth ("in his holy sanctuary") and those already in heaven ("in his stronghold in the sky") are a part of a great cloud of witnesses who praise the Lord together for his glorious deeds.

## Why Should We Praise God?

• *Read Psalm 150:2. For what reasons should we praise God?*

• *What "mighty miracles" has he performed in your life? How has he shown his "magnificent greatness"?*

# How Should We Praise God?

Read verses 3–5. Elsewhere the Bible tells us to "Make a joyful noise" to the Lord (Psalm 66:1 KJV).

- *What musical instrument could you add to this scene? If you can't play an instrument, how could you join in anyhow?*

- *When was the last time you worshiped God as enthusiastically as the participants in the worship service described here?*

- *How does your worship typically reflect the joy that is in your heart?*

## Who Should Joyfully Praise God?

- *Read Psalm 150:6. Not everyone everywhere is willing to praise the Lord currently, but one day, who will bow before him? For help, check out Romans 14:10–12 and Philippians 2:10.*

# THE BACKSTORY

Read 2 Samuel 6:12–23. David was in a rejoicing mood. After many months, the ark of the Lord was finally returning to its rightful place in Jerusalem, and King David could not contain his joy. As the ark was being carried into the city, David was overcome, and he danced passionately, vigorously, "with all his might" (KJV) before God, entirely unconcerned with what other people thought—including his wife Michal, the daughter of the previous king, Saul.

- *How would you have responded if you were Michal?*

- *Why did David have no concern for what others thought of his expression of praise to God?*

- *Some people prefer a wilder, ecstatic, more passionate form of worship. Others love the reverence and majesty of the older hymns of the church. Which do you prefer and why? How do both forms of worship have a place in the body of Christ?*

# ⓝ WORD WEALTH

Christians everywhere are familiar with the great exclamation of praise: "Hallelujah!" It is actually a Hebrew word that means "praise to Yahweh (or God)."[37]

- *The first and last lines of this psalm contain the word "Hallelujah." How is this a fitting format for this concluding song in the book of Psalms?*

- *Saint Augustine of Hippo said, "A Christian should be a Hallelujah from head to foot."[38] How is the "hallelujah" of praise exhibited in your life "from head to foot"?*

- *How could you cause a "hallelujah" to begin and end each of your days?*

# ♥ EXPERIENCE GOD'S HEART

- *What aspects of worship do you see in this psalm that you would like to incorporate into your own times of praise and worship? How could you begin to do so?*

Psalm 150:4–5 tells us to worship God with the "loud clashing of cymbals!" When our praise is genuine and comes from a sincere heart, this is a beautiful sound in God's ears. Even a cacophony of discordant sound becomes a "joyful noise" to the Lord!

- *When might this sound not be pleasant to God (see 1 Corinthians 13:1)?*

• *What is the key to pleasing God in your worship?*

## ❤ SHARE GOD'S HEART

As you live a life of worship before others, they will naturally be drawn to the God whom you so obviously adore. But the same applies as we praise God before others—without love in our actions, our worship seems hollow, and our ministry looks more like hypocrisy.

• *How can a genuine adoration of God spill over into our treatment of our fellow human beings?*

- *Read all of 1 Corinthians 13. What can you do today to praise the Lord through your love and service to others?*

# Talking It Out

1. What is your favorite praise and worship song? Or perhaps you have a favorite hymn that you love. What about this song makes it your favorite? If possible, share the song with your small group or a friend and worship God together.

2. Where, when, and how do you usually praise God? How would it feel to try something different? What might that be?

3. The New Testament tells us that we have a great cloud of witnesses in heaven (Hebrews 12:1)—and that our praises here on earth join theirs around God's throne. Whom do you know who is now worshiping God in heaven? How does it feel to know that you are still connected to that person through your worship of God?

4. What did you learn in this study that most stands out to you? How will it make a difference in your walk with God moving forward? What lessons will you commit to living out from now on?

# Endnotes

1. Brian Simmons et al., "A Note to Readers," *The Passion Translation: The New Testament with Psalms, Proverbs, and Song of Songs* (Savage, MN: BroadStreet Publishing Group, 2020), ix.

2. James Strong, *Strong's Exhaustive Concordance of the Bible*, Hebrew #4210.

3. Psalm 3:2, note 'd,' TPT.

4. "St. Athanasius—The Psalms Seem to Me," *Catholic Digest*, accessed February 27, 2022, https://www.catholicdigest.com/from-the-magazine/quiet-moment/st-athanasius-the-psalms-seem-to-me.

5. John Calvin, *John Calvin's Commentaries on the Psalms, Volume 1* (Grand Rapids: Kregel Academic, 2016), 205.

6. Dwight L. Moody, quoted in William M. Anderson, *The Faith That Satisfies* (New York: Loizeaux Brothers, 1949), 165.

7. Jock Purves, *Fair Sunshine* (London: Banner of Truth, 1968), 17.

8   R. Laird Harris, Gleason L. Archer Jr., and Bruce K. Waltke, eds., *Theological Wordbook of the Old Testament*, 2 vols. (Chicago: Moody Press, 1980), vol. 1, s.v. "hesed," #698a.

9   Clark Cothern, "I Saw Something Different in Those Guys," *Decision* magazine, May 2000, 18.

10  Timothy Ferris, *Coming of Age in the Milky Way* (New York: William Morrow, 1988), 383.

11  Arthur Conan Doyle, *The Adventure of the Naval Treaty* (Birmingham, MI: Strand, 1993), 59.

12  Bob Reccord, *Forged by Fire* (Nashville: Broadman & Holman, 2000), 145.

13  Elizabeth Barrett Browning, *Aurora Leigh* (Oxford: Oxford University Press, 2008), bk. 7, lines 61–64.

14  Lawrence O. Richards, *Expository Dictionary of Bible Words* (Grand Rapids, MI: Zondervan, 1985), s.v. "Anointing/Anointed."

15  Psalm 22:20, note 'c,' TPT.

16  J. Barton Payne, *The Encyclopedia of Biblical Prophecy: The Complete Guide to Scriptural Predictions and Their Fulfillment* (New York: Harper & Row, 1973), 665–70, 682.

17  Josh McDowell, *The New Evidence That Demands a Verdict* (Nashville: Thomas Nelson, 1999), 87.

18  Psalm 103:14, note 'b,' TPT.

19  Clarence Edward Macartney, *Preaching without Notes* (Nashville: Abingdon-Cokesbury Press, 1946), 148.

20  John Alexander, *The Other Side* magazine, Issue 150, Vol. 20, 1, March 1984, 46.

21  Psalm 51:10, note 'c,' TPT.

22  Psalm 51:9, note 'b,' TPT.

23  Margo Howard, *Ann Landers in Her Own Words* (New York: Grand Central, 2005), 5.

24  Billy Graham, *Angels* (Nashville: Thomas Nelson, 1995), 37.

25  C. Fred Dickason, *Angels: Elect and Evil* (Chicago: Moody Press, 1975), 92, 98–99.

26  See Psalm 91:1, note 'd,' TPT.

27  Psalm 23:1, note 'c,' TPT.

28  *Strong's Exhaustive Concordance of the Bible*, Hebrew #3176.

29  Paul Thigpen, "Where's the Joy?" *Discipleship Journal*, May/June 1996, 21.

30  Norman P. Grubb, *C. T. Studd, Cricketer and Pioneer* (London: Religious Tract Society, 1933), 52–53.

31  "The Dick Staub Interview: Brennan Manning on Ruthless Trust," ChristianityToday.com, December 1, 2002, https://www.christianitytoday.com/ct/2002/decemberweb-only/12-9-21.0.html.

32  Zig Ziglar, "Zig Ziglar Quote," AZ Quotes, accessed February 27, 2022, https://www.azquotes.com/quote/826893.

33  Angela K. Troyer, "Spaced Repetition,"
    *Psychology Today*, March 31, 2014, https://www.
    psychologytoday.com/us/blog/living-mild-cognitive-
    impairment/201403/spaced-repetition?amp.

34  Charles Colson and Ellen Santilli Vaughn, *The Body:
    Being Light in the Darkness* (Dallas: Word Publishing,
    1992), 32.

35  "Christian Persecution," *Open Doors*, accessed
    February 27, 2022, https://www.opendoorsusa.org/
    christian-persecution.

36  Open Doors at opendoorsusa.com is one of several
    organizations dedicated to this contemporary problem
    and striving to address it. You can find ample
    opportunities for prayer, information, giving, and
    other forms of involvement through their websites.

37  *Strong's Exhaustive Concordance of the Bible*, Hebrew
    #239.

38  Saint Augustine, "Praise," Tony Cook Ministries,
    accessed June 9, 2022, https://tonycooke.org/quotes/
    quote6/#P.